Praise for *Every Child R*

"*Every Child Ready to Read* is a little gem. It will help parents prepare, support, guide, and enjoy reading with their children. Nothing could be a better gift to any new family."

—SUSAN STRAUB, director, Read to Me program

"Lee Pesky would have been so proud of the work of the Lee Pesky Center and even more proud of the book they have written— *Every Child Ready to Read*. This book will help all parents. Having a child with a learning disability, I know the importance of early stimulation of a child's mind. I personally would have loved to have had this book twenty years ago!"

—ANNE FORD, author of *Laughing Allegra*, and chairman emeritus, National Center for Learning Disabilities

"*Every Child Ready to Read* is a wonderful guide for parents of young children, chock full of helpful advice that's just right for getting a child started on a lifetime of reading."

—SALLY E. SHAYWITZ, M.D., professor of pediatrics, codirector, Yale Center for the Study of Learning and Attention

"This is a clear, practical guide to raising young readers, full of ideas that any parent can apply. It goes well beyond the usual sound advice ('read to your child') by highlighting the importance of oral language, music, and creative play."

—NOEL GUNTHER, WETA

"Because learning to read was difficult for me as a dyslexic child, I appreciate more than most the value and joy of reading. From now on, *Every Child Ready to Read* will be the baby present I give. The Lee Pesky Learning Center has created a valuable resource for parents. Teaching our children to read, especially when they face obstacles, is one of the most important gifts we can give them."

—GOVERNOR GASTON CAPERTON, former governor of West Virginia and president of The College Board

"Do not underestimate the value of this book for parents and care-givers alike. We only wish it had been available twenty-plus years ago for our children's benefit. The Lee Pesky Learning Center, its founders, its directors and the legacy it represents and perpetuates is to be commended and celebrated. Thank you for your sincere love of learning, literacy and little ones."

—GOVERNOR DIRK KEMPTHORNE and
FIRST LADY PATRICIA KEMPTHORNE of Idaho

"Every Child Ready to Read can make a real difference in the lives of children and their parents."

—PAUL FIRSTENBERG,
former chief operating officer, *Sesame Street*

Every Child Ready to Read

Literacy Tips
for
Parents

The Lee Pesky Learning Center

Ballantine Books
New York

A Ballantine Book
Published by The Random House Publishing Group

Copyright © 2004 by The Lee Pesky Learning Center

www.ballantinebooks.com

Cataloging-in-Publication Data is available from the Library of Congress.

ISBN: 0-345-47067-2

This book published by arrangement with Random House, Inc.

Text design by Mary A. Wirth

Manufactured in the United States of America
First Edition: August 2004

2   4   6   8   9   7   5   3   1

*No parent should expect more from their child
than to have them fulfill their full potential in life.
There is nothing more critical in helping this
become a reality than being able to read.*

*It is our hope that this book will assist parents
in making it possible to have their
children achieve this goal.*

—*Alan and Wendy Pesky*

Preface

Tell Me a Story?

Children love stories. As adults, some of our most cherished memories are of being read to as a child and of carrying on this legacy as we read to our own child. *Every Child Ready to Read* is the outcome of a story—of the Alan and Wendy Pesky family and their beloved son Lee. And so we decided to begin this book with the once-upon-a-time of how this book came to be. This is a true story with very real people just like you and me.

Once upon a time, really quite a long time ago, there was a dark-haired, laughing little boy named Lee Pesky. He had a father, Alan, a mother, Wendy, an older sister, Heidi, and a younger brother, Greg. They lived in Connecticut. Often they traveled to Idaho, where they skied, rafted on the rivers, and went camping. Lee really liked Sun Valley.

Lee was very smart; however, reading and writing were a mystery. School was very difficult for Lee, and he did not like it. He struggled to read and write. It was so hard! Lee felt scared and mad. Lee had a very good brain, but it worked differently.

When Lee was growing up in the 1970s we did not know much about learning differently or learning disabilities. The Pesky family was worried. They wanted to find out as much as they could to help Lee love reading and learning as much as he loved to hike and camp. They searched and searched for help.

Finally they found a neurologist who helped Lee and his family understand how Lee's brain worked. Lee was able to get the help he needed to read, learn, and enjoy school. As Lee got ready to enter college, he worked with Dr. Sally Shaywitz on issues relating to his learning problems so that he could do his best in college.

When Lee graduated from college, he returned to Idaho and started a bagel business in Ketchum. It was a funny little store, and Lee named it Buckin' Bagels. The business grew, and he opened another store in Boise. Everyone loved Lee's bagels. Buckin' Bagels was a great success. Lee planned to open several other stores around the state.

Lee was still very young when he became ill and died. The Pesky family wanted to create something in Lee's name—a gift that would keep Lee's memory and spirit alive. They decided to found the Lee Pesky Learning Center in Boise, Idaho, in 1997.

The center works with students of all ages who struggle with learning disabilities. Thanks to neuroscientists such as Dr. Sally Shaywitz and Dr. Bennett there is a lot of information now about how our brains develop and learn. We know that babies come into the world learning from every experience they have. We have learned that brains are learning and growing from the moment of birth. We know that talking and reading to young children help them get ready to learn to read when they go to kindergarten.

And we know that there are "all kinds of minds," as Mel Levine has stated. We know how to help all kinds of minds learn to read, write, and do math. Since the center opened, we have worked with hundreds of students. Lee's mother, Wendy, says, "Every time a student leaves the center, I feel a little bit of Lee goes with them."

The center is located in Boise, Idaho, because Lee loved Idaho. Many different people work at the center. We have psychologists who do assessments to identify how a student learns. We have educational specialists who work with center students. We have a staff who designs curriculum and training programs for schools. And we work with many foundations that are interested in education and learning disabilities.

One of these foundations, the Dumke Foundation, gave the center funding to develop early literacy materials. Early literacy means understanding that reading and talking with infants and preschoolers can help them be ready to read. Reading this story about Lee Pesky helps you get ready to go to school. We are learning about how to hold a book. We are learning about words and sentences. We are learning that words have letters. So many things we are learning. There are many games, activities, and other fun things that parents, grandparents, babysitters, and preschool teachers can do to help you—yes, *you*—get ready to read.

All the staff of the Lee Pesky Learning Center worked together to create *Every Child Ready to Read* and Kathleen Odean, author of *Great Books for Babies and Toddlers* prepared the booklists. The book was first printed as *Literacy Tips for Parents for the Beginnings* (Federal Early Literacy Summit for the Northwest Region). Mrs. Laura Bush and the many researchers who came to the meeting liked the book and wanted as many parents as possible to have it. Because being ready to read is the most important thing you can do to be ready for school. Now *Literacy Tips for Parents* will go to bookstores all across the country as *Every Child Ready to Read* so that children and their families can get ready to read. And in each book is a little bit of Lee Pesky helping you get ready to read.

Hildegarde Ayer
EXECUTIVE DIRECTOR
The Lee Pesky Learning Center

Acknowledgments

Our thanks to the Lee Pesky Learning Center Staff: Sue Shiele, Sharon Bixby, Margo Healy, Jeri Jessup, Tracy Holloway, Mitzi Hunt, and Mary Goff. And to Kathleen Odean, Alan and Wendy Pesky, the Ezekiel and Edna Wattis Dumke Foundation, the Idaho Community Foundation, and the Whittenberger Foundation.

Contents

How to Use
This Book

Reading is a significant tool in life's journey, and helping your child develop reading readiness skills is a priceless lifetime gift. Reading is also a great joy. It provides a time for reverie and imagination, and reading to a child provides a special time for cuddling, for talking, for storytelling, for attachment. By reading to our children, we expand our horizons and our perspective. We understand other worlds, other people, and other beliefs.

The literacy tips you will find in this book are not intended to teach your child to read. That will happen in school. The early years from infancy to preschool are a time of preparation and support so that your child begins kindergarten ready to learn to read. Early literacy, as suggested here, uses the daily activities of parenting and caregiving to help you knowledgably guide the natural learning energy of your child. Through the opportunities of playtime, bath time, and bedtime you can create enjoyable experiences that promote reading readiness.

Every Child Ready to Read is built on the recognition that the simple acts of talking and reading build vocabulary, the awareness that letters have sounds and that words are made up of letters, and an understanding of how to hold a book. These are the keys to helping your child get ready to learn to read.

What Is Early Learning?

Research has provided significant information on brain development and learning. New studies are appearing every day on the importance of your role, as parent, grandparent or other caregiver. (For information on specific studies, see www.schwablearning.org—a parents' guide to helping kids with learning difficulties—or www.talaris.org/timeline.) You are a child's first teacher, and you can utilize the day's activities of home, family, and community life to help your child start school ready to learn to read. Something as simple as an infant showing excitement over pictures in a storybook, or a two-year-old scribbling in a coloring book is a signal of a child's growing literacy development.

Children enter our world as tiny bundles of learning energy. Parents, grandparents, nannies, and other caretakers marvel as infants coo, babies grab, toddlers climb and explore. We love to watch and experience our children's development. In these early years your child is learning the physical basics—from rolling over to standing, crawling, walking, running, and climbing! Watch your child test what works and what doesn't—the intensity of the effort to become more mobile. We can clearly see how one physical development leads to another. The milestones, the stimuli, the setbacks, and the next new steps are transparent—indeed, the cause of many a memorable and celebratory moment. All of you no doubt vividly recall your child's first step. We instinctively act to keep our children's explorations safe. We can see their vulnerability and we know what to do—we place plugs in our outlets and remove dangerous items from cupboards and tabletops.

Just so, the infant brain develops thinking, processing, communication, and response skills. These are not as readily visible. We cannot *see* the brain develop. We cannot *see* how and in what ways our child's brain is growing and learning. The neuroscientific research of the past decade has enriched our awareness of what is happening with the developing brain, underscored the critical and determinative impact of early childhood experience, and helped us to more effectively utilize our caregiving to promote our child's learning and development. Dr. Patricia Kuhl, co-director of the University of Washington Institute for Mind, Brain, and Learning has demonstrated that by age six months, a baby's brain has organized sounds into categories associated with the language of his/her environment. We now know that the interchange of cooing and baby talk between parent and infant is instrumental to the evolving language skills of the child. In 1999, the National Reading Panel reported that "talking to adults is children's best source of exposure to new vocabulary and ideas."

We know, for example, that some children start school with a vocabulary of over ten thousand words. Others start school with a small vocabulary of three thousand words. We know that children who start school with a sizable working vocabulary have a tremendous progress and achievement advantage over those with limited vocabularies. This advantage continues through the years of the child's education. The more you talk and read with your child, the better prepared your child will be to begin school excited and ready to learn. Children who start school with readiness skills are demonstrably ahead in their progress and achievement.

How does the brain develop? What happens with early learning? How can you as a parent understand this process? Brain development is a marvelous, indeed miraculous process, and many of you will want to know and learn much more. *Every Child Ready to Read* includes a number of excellent references. (See in particular Jack P. Shonkoff, ed., *From Neurons to Neighborhoods* and Alison Gopnik, Andrew N. Meltzoff, and Patricia K. Kuhl, *The Scientist in the Crib*.)

A child's brain will form trillions of connections or synapses in the first decade of life. In the first three years of life the speed of formation is particularly exuberant and robust. The connections are formed through the growing child's experience of the surrounding world and developing attachments with parents and other caretakers. If these connections are used repeatedly in a child's day-to-day life, they are reinforced and form part of the permanent circuitry of the brain. If they are not used repeatedly or frequently, they are eliminated in a process called pruning.

This is the learning process. Your child is learning by forming connections! What you do with your child informs, guides, and supports this learning process. The pace of growth is fast and furious, particularly in the first few years of your child's life, when your child's accumulation of impressions and conclusions from early experience and relationships is intense. As parents, caregivers, and members of a community, we are faced with an awesome responsibility to support this process. What we do and how frequently we do it guides our children's learning.

For parents who bemusedly wonder if their active two-year-old might possibly be smarter than they are—have no doubt! The answer is unequivocally yes in terms of raw neuronal mass and speed of learning. The research tells us that age birth to five is a decisive developmental period of "learning to learn." In these years your child develops the prerequisites—the readiness skills for the more formalized learning of school and community.

Why Is Literacy Readiness Important?

Literacy has been categorized by the National Center for Child Health and Development as a public health problem. Over 40 percent of the children in the United States are not reading at grade level by the end of the third grade. For minority children the percentage is much larger. We know that children who are not reading at grade level as they begin the fourth grade are at great risk for not catching up. It is more costly and takes much longer to remediate a struggling reader in the upper elementary and middle grades.

We also know that a struggling reader at the junior high or high school level cannot comprehend the classroom instruction—competency in literacy is essential to content mastery as one advances in the educational system. Literacy competency is largely assumed in the junior high and high school years. Faced with standards and exit exams, struggling students may well join the ranks of dropouts. These numbers and consequences undermine the social and economic health of our society.

How Will *Every Child Ready to Read* Help Me?

Parents want to give their young children the strongest foundation to prepare them for later success in reading and writing. *Every Child Ready to Read: Literacy Tips for Parents* provides tools to foster the kind of learning that best prepares young children for learning to read when the time comes. Here you will find useful activities, book lists, and information divided into chapters addressing three age groups: infants (birth to eighteen months), toddlers (eighteen to thirty-six months), and preschoolers (three and four years).

Each age group chapter is organized around four key pillars of learning, with specific advice about each aspect of learning for that age group and enjoyable activities to reinforce the learning. The first pillar, oral language and vocabulary, concerns creating an environment in which children are exposed to lots of spoken language and a varied vocabulary. This sort of language-rich environment is a strong indicator of a child's future reading skills in school.

The second, awareness of the sounds of the language, emphasizes to children the fact that each word consists of different combinations of sounds. Letter knowledge, which means knowing the names of letters and the sounds they represent, is the third pillar. Both of these pillars of learning are important predictors of early reading success. Print awareness, the fourth aspect, refers to the understanding that print—those mysterious marks on the page—carries information or a story.

These four aspects of literacy develop gradually over time, beginning with infants and expanding for toddlers and preschoolers. The four pillars overlap, and the activities you do to encourage development in one area will help in the other areas as well.

Following the three age-group chapters comes a short discussion of learning disabilities, including a description of warning signs and helpful resources. Estimates suggest that one in five individuals has a learning disability, with a common manifestation being difficulty with reading. Awareness of the warning signs and early detection make it possible to provide intervention for a child as early as preschool.

A final chapter provides parents with resources, including tips on where and how to read aloud, magazines for young children, award-winning books with outstanding art, children's books in Spanish, advice on using public libraries, helpful Web sites and organizations, and books for further reading.

Keep in mind that the early literacy activities described in the following pages give children wonderful learning experiences, but they work best as an enjoyable time together rather than as lessons. Aim to share a comfortable, stress-free interlude with your child, reading a book, singing songs, and drawing pictures.

Have a special place where you and your child can snuggle and read together. Remember, every child has a different attention span. Follow your child's lead. If he or she tires of an activity, shorten it and move on to something else. You can promote a love of learning and a longer attention span with patience and calmness.

Above all, have fun reading together, singing, and doing these activities with your child!

The Pesky Family and the staff of the Lee Pesky Learning Center hope this book will help you prepare your child for a world of reading. We believe that *each individual's triumph in learning is a victory for our world.*

Every Child
Ready to Read

1

Infants
Birth to Eighteen Months

Readers aren't born, they're made.
Desire is planted—planted by parents who work at it.
—Jim Trelease

For children from birth to eighteen months, parents help build a solid foundation for future learning simply by cuddling and rocking their babies and singing and cooing to them. From birth on, infants are connected to human beings and prefer looking at faces over anything else in their environment. Babies respond joyfully to the sound of the human voice and love to hear "parent-ese." Experts in brain research stress that touch helps to build a baby's brain. Babies love to feel gentle touches on the arms, legs, tummy, and face. They notice and imitate facial expressions at just a few months of age. Begin talking to babies the moment they are born, listen to them babble and coo, and imitate the sounds they produce.

While children develop at somewhat different rates, experts offer overall milestones regarding literacy development. By twelve months, most children will sit on a parent's lap to share a book, reach for a nearby book, enjoy looking at pictures, and turn pages in board books with help from an adult.

By eighteen months, typically a child can hold a book with help, turn pages in a board book (usually several at a time), turn a book right side up, point to favorite pictures, and point to a picture of a familiar object when it's named. Children this age often carry a book to an adult, indicating they'd like to have it read.

Activities to Promote Oral Language and Vocabulary

• Carry on "conversations" with infants. Notice how they listen and respond during pauses. Show lots of facial expression, especially smiles, while playing with infants.

• Show babies items in their environment and name them. Name and talk about the cat, blanket, chair, and rug. This helps children to learn that everything has a name.

• Speak "parent-ese," talking with exaggerated changes in pitch and stretching out words.

• Play the bag game. Put six to eight small toys or household objects (larger than two to three inches to avoid choking potential) in a container. Try things like toy cars, wooden spoons, measuring spoons, and coasters. Allow your baby to pull items out and explore them. Tell her the name of the object and join in the play. Describe an action such as "I am putting the red coaster under the car."

Always follow your baby's lead, and don't force an activity. If your baby grows tired of a game, choose another one or stop for the time being.

Traditional Games

- Pat-a-cake and peekaboo may seem like simple games, but brain researchers tell us that babies are learning a lot when they play them. Games are very important for wiring the brain; they promote cognitive growth by strengthening and making brain-cell connections.

- The most common way to play peekaboo is to cover your face with your hands and take them away, saying "Peekaboo, I see you!"

- You can also hold a blanket up between you and the baby, peeking out around the edge or dropping the top, and saying the magic words.

- Once they sit up, some babies like to have a small blanket tossed over their head so they can take it off to peek at you.

- To teach pat-a-cake, put your baby on your lap, hold his hands, and gently guide him through the actions as you recite the poem. He will enjoy showing off the new skill as the days go by. Here is one version of the rhyme:

  Pat-a-cake, pat-a-cake, baker's man
  (*Clap baby's hands gently together*)
  Bake me a cake as fast as you can
  (*Clap to the beat*)

Roll it and pat it
 (Roll hands, then pat the baby's stomach)
And mark it with a B
 (Draw a B on baby's stomach)
And put it in the oven for baby and me
 (Point to baby and to self)

Have fun. Remember that babies and young children learn through play.

Activities to Promote Your Child's Awareness of the Sounds of Language

- Encourage any activity that plays with sounds. Play peekaboo using scarves, puppets, or objects in bags. Vary the sounds you make as you say "peekaboo": "ah," "oo," "ee."

- Notice and imitate the rhythm of your baby's cooing.

- Create original verses about your baby's actions and set them to traditional tunes. For example, substitute "Here We Go to Grandmother's House" for "Here We Go Round the Mulberry Bush," or "Are You Crawling?" for "Are You Sleeping?"

- Choose one or two rhymes to croon to your baby before bedtime. She will begin to associate that rhyme with getting sleepy.

Recommended Nursery Rhyme and Fingerplay Books

A book of nursery rhymes makes an ideal baby-shower gift, ensuring that parents will have something to read to their newborn, moving straight into the habit of reading aloud. Nursery rhymes—often called Mother Goose rhymes—have been around for hundreds of years and suit young children perfectly thanks to their brevity and irresistible rhythms. Even if you don't remember any from your childhood, you'll soon memorize some of these quick verses and can use them to entertain your child at any time of day. The following list suggests some wonderful collections as well as some single rhymes illustrated with inviting pictures.

Some rhymes, dubbed fingerplays, have finger, hand, or body movements that go with them. While you might already know pat-a-cake or "This Little Piggy," collections on this list will give you new ideas and lead to new favorites. Start by performing the fingerplays for your infant and note the delight on his face. Then, as he gets a bit older, your toddler will naturally join in the words and movements.

Beaton, Clare. *Mother Goose Remembers.*
Stunning cloth art illustrates this charming collection of forty-six familiar nursery rhymes, which makes a great baby-shower gift.

Baker, Keith. *Big Fat Hen.*
A lot happens in the engaging pictures of hens and a barn-yard, set to the words and rhythms of a familiar nursery rhyme, which opens, "one, two, buckle my shoe."

Brown, Marc. *Finger Rhymes.*
This attractive collection gives the words and actions for fingerplays, some that may be familiar and others less well known. Look also for Brown's *Hand Rhymes* and *Play Rhymes.*

Cousins, Lucy. *Humpty Dumpty and Other Nursery Rhymes.*
A sturdy, brightly colored board book with several well-chosen nursery rhymes.

Cole, Joanna, and Stephanie Calmenson, compilers. *Pat-a-Cake and Other Play Rhymes.* **Illustrated by Alan Tiegreen.**
Here's a valuable cornucopia of interactive rhymes, includ-ing fingerplays, bouncing rhymes, tickling rhymes, and more.

dePaola, Tomie. *Tomie dePaola's Mother Goose.*
This large collection brings together more than two hun-dred traditional rhymes, accompanied by tidy illustrations in delicious colors.

Dunn, Opal. *Hippety-Hop Hippety-Hay: Growing with Rhymes from Birth to Age Three.* Illustrated by Sally Anne Lambert.
Another fine collection, this also tells new parents what to expect at different ages in terms of listening and language acquisition.

Manning, Jane. *My First Baby Games.*
This handy little book offers seven time-tested rhymes perfect for chanting to infants while performing the matching movements.

Opie, Iona, editor. *My Very First Mother Goose.*
Illustrated by Rosemary Wells.
A gem among Mother Goose books, this oversized collection offers page after page of charming illustrations. A wonderful baby shower gift that will delight a child for years.

Westcott, Nadine Bernard, adapter. *The Lady with the Alligator Purse.*
Read this bouncing rhyme to your baby—or to an older child. Nobody can resist the catchy verses and the witty pictures.

Make Music a Part of Daily Life

Music is another way children are introduced to sound and, in most musical recordings, to words. Brain research indicates that singing to babies facilitates bonding between adult and child. The following pages suggest musical recordings to try with infants and toddlers. Also check out the list of songbooks on pages 26 and 27.

Diaper Songs
• Singing to your baby while you change a diaper is a wonderful way to communicate and bond with her.

• Smile while you are singing.

• Sing any song you know, or sing the following to the tune of "This is the way we . . ." (which can be used at any time of day by changing the lyrics to fit the activity):

This is the way we change your diaper
Change your diaper
Change your diaper
This is the way we change your diaper
And now you're clean and dry—hey!

Musical Recordings for Babies and Toddlers

Jessica Harper. *40 Winks.* **Alacazam.**
An award-winning recording, this will please parents as well as young children.

Various Artists. *American Lullaby.* **Ellipsis Arts.**
Sweet Honey in the Rock, Bill Staines, Maria Muldaur, and others sing lullabies.

Sally Rogers. *At Quiet O'Clock.* **Rounder.**
Lullabies with piano, guitar, and dulcimer accompaniments, this is a wonderful baby gift.

Susie Tallman. *Classic Nursery Rhymes.* **Rock Me Baby Records.**
Remind yourself of familiar nursery rhyme tunes and learn new ones from this fine collection.

Steve Rashid. *I Will Hold Your Tiny Hand: Evening Songs and Lullabies.* **Woodside Avenue Music.**
Don't limit these great songs to bedtime, but listen to them whenever quiet music fits your child's day.

Various Artists. *Mozart Effect: Music for Babies from Playtime to Sleepytime.* **Children's Group.**
A variety of Mozart's music chosen especially to soothe young children.

Various Artists. *On a Starry Night.* **Windham Hill.**
Artists from Bobby McFerrin to George Winston contributed their favorite lullaby to this lovely recording.

Mr. Al. *Rock the Baby.* **Melody House**
Gentle lullabies, tunes that include movements, and funny songs come together in this excellent recording.

Raffi. *Singable Songs for the Very Young.* **Rounder.**
A classic recording with lots of childhood favorites, from perhaps the most popular performer for children.

Ella Jenkins. *You'll Sing a Song and I'll Sing a Song.*
Smithsonian Folkways.
The pacing of these songs makes them perfect for sing-a-longs.

Activities to Help Your Child Learn About Letters and Become Aware of Print

- Show your baby pictures with high contrast, such as simple black-and-white drawings of faces, dogs, cats, or other familiar images.

- Place colorful letters and numbers on your baby's bedroom wall.

- Sing the alphabet song.

- Monitor for ear infections. Chronic ear infections can cause difficulties in discriminating the sounds of the language. Have your child see a doctor regularly.

- Help develop your baby's vision by moving a small, colorful toy back and forth across her field of vision, encouraging her to follow it, saying, "Where is Froggy? He's over here. Now he's going down to your tummy."

- Read often to infants for short periods of time, using lots of expression. Read your baby's favorites over and over again.

- Allow your baby to hold the book once she is sitting and grasping.

- Watch to see what pictures she is interested in. Stop and talk about them.

Recommended Books for Birth to Eighteen Months

In choosing books for this age group, look for pictures with simple shapes, bright colors, and sharp contrast that make it easy for very young children to make sense of the pictures. The texts should also be uncomplicated, with a limited number of words. Rhyme, rhythm, and repetition all appeal to babies and toddlers. Simple stories about familiar things work well, as do books where familiar objects are named. Books about animals and vehicles provide a perfect chance for parents to make noises that invite children to join in. And even the youngest child is fascinated by a book with flaps to move (or watch an adult move) and textures to touch. Since young children treat books like toys, look for small board books that can be easily wiped clean. Finally, don't forget the nursery rhyme and fingerplay books described earlier.

Ahlberg, Janet, and Allan Ahlberg. *Baby Sleeps*.
This small book has a picture of a baby on every page and brief text such as "Baby bounces" and "Baby hides."

Boynton, Sandra. *Blue Hat, Green Hat*.
This little book delights parents and children with its humorous story about a bird who puts on clothes the wrong way. One of many popular books by Boynton.

Charlip, Remy. *Sleepytime Rhyme.*
This ode, which has a gentle rhythm and lovely pictures, can be sung to the tune of "Twinkle, Twinkle, Little Star."

Hoban, Tana. *Black on White.*
Since infants respond visually to contrast and patterns, this small black-and-white book suits them with its silhouettes of familiar objects. The companion book is *White on Black.*

Hubbell, Patricia. *Pots and Pans.* **Illustrated by Diane de Groat.**
Watch out! Baby's found the pot and pan cupboard and is having a great time banging and clanging.

Ormerod, Jan. *Peek-a-Boo!*
This book echoes the game of peekaboo, with the question "Where's the baby?" and flaps that hide smiling faces.

Oxenbury, Helen. *All Fall Down.*
Larger than most board books, this shows plump babies with different skin colors tumbling around together. Companion books are *Clap Hands, Say Goodnight,* and *Tickle Tickle.*

Pinkney, Andrea, and Brian Pinkney. *Shake Shake Shake.*
A mother, daughter, and little brother make music with a shekere, an African percussion instrument. Also look for *Pretty Brown Face* and *Watch Me Dance.*

Rowe, Jeannette. *Whose Ears?*
In this brightly illustrated guessing book, the question "Whose ears?" is repeated, while a flap hides all but the ears of an animal.

Taylor, Ann. *Baby Dance.* **Illustrated by Marjorie van Heerden.**
The words in this lovely board book sing from beginning to end as a black father dances with his baby girl.

Touch and Feel Kitten.
One in a popular series of small books, this incorporates different textures for children to touch into photographs of cute kittens.

Tracy, Tom. *Show Me!* **Illustrated by Darcia Labrosse.**
A mother plays a simple game with her baby, pointing out and naming the baby's nose, cheek, chin, and more.

Gift Ideas for Infants

Active Play
• Stacking blocks made of foam and soft cloth
• Brightly colored blankets and mats for crawling on
• Mobiles to place above the crib or on the changing table

Dolls and Pretend Play
• Stuffed animals of various sizes
• Soft cuddly dolls
• Puppets

Manipulatives
• Rattles, musical balls
• Manipulable crib boards that attach to the side of a crib, with knobs, buttons, and slides for a child to operate

Art Gifts
• Bright pictures and posters of nursery rhymes, nature scenes, or favorite literary characters

Books and Music
• Board books with large, simple pictures
• Tapes and CDs of lullabies
• Soft cloth books

2

Toddlers

Ages Eighteen to Thirty-Six Months

> When an infant shows excitement over pictures in a
> storybook, when a two-year-old scribbles with a crayon,
> when a four-year-old points out letters in a street sign—all of
> these actions signal a child's growing literacy development.
> —*The National Research Council*

Language development flourishes in children ages eighteen to thirty-six months. By sixteen months, children
are adding to their vocabularies daily, and most two-year-
olds have vocabularies of fifty to three hundred words.
Daily story reading is critical for both language development and print understanding; young children who are
exposed to books are motivated to learn about how print
carries meaning. Spend time every day talking with your
child, labeling actions and feelings, and naming pictures
and new objects. Talk together while driving in the car,

visiting the zoo, looking at books, or taking a bath, and include toddlers in mealtime conversations.

While children develop at somewhat different rates, experts offer overall milestones regarding literacy development. By twenty-four months, a child can typically turn pages in a board book one at a time, name familiar objects in pictures, fill in some words in familiar stories, and pretend to read to stuffed animals or dolls. Children this age often carry a book around the house, just for fun or hoping to be read to.

By thirty-six months, a child can typically recite phrases from favorite stories, or even most of the story; she can pretend to read to herself and is learning to turn paper pages. Children this age often object if a parent skips or substitutes words in a familiar story.

Activities to Promote Oral Language and Vocabulary

• Play games to promote language and vocabulary. Make up a story and have the child fill in the blanks, like this, "Once upon a time there was a girl named ____. She liked to ____."

• Demonstrate storytelling while building with blocks or other construction toys, or playing with dolls or action characters. You might say something like, "My name is Bill. I live in this castle, and there's a dragon in the dungeon."

• Move stuffed animals from place to place, saying, "Where is Fluffy?" Encourage your toddler to use spatial terms, such as *under* the tree, *in* the basement, or *behind* the castle.

• Help your child learn words that describe emotions: *happy, sad, sorry, shy, angry, frustrated, excited*. Look in a mirror and make faces together or cut out pictures from magazines that show different emotions. Use a variety of words to describe the emotions you see.

Bath Time

Bath time with an infant, toddler, or preschooler is filled with opportunities for rich learning. Provide cups, simple toys such as rubber ducks, and sponges and washcloths for play and experimentation.

Hold your baby firmly and guide him through the water like a boat while singing:

Row, row, row your boat
Gently down the stream
Merrily, merrily, merrily, merrily
Life is but a dream

Activities to Promote Your Child's Awareness of the Sounds of Language

- Chant fingerplays or action rhymes to your child. With this one, you can touch your baby's head, shoulders, and so on. As a child gets older, he or she will join in with the words and actions. Find more in the books listed on pages 9–11.

   Head, shoulders, knees and toes, knees and toes
   Head, shoulders, knees and toes, knees and toes
   Eyes and ears and mouth and nose
   Head, shoulders, knees and toes, knees and toes

- Read lots of rhyming books and books that play with the language, including nursery rhyme books.

- Share a book with a strong rhythm or a nursery rhyme, and encourage your child to clap to the beat of the words.

- Play simple rhyming games with your toddler. Gather small objects, toys, or pictures of objects whose names rhyme, such as *cat, hat,* and *bat; sock, rock,* and *clock; rice, mice,* and *dice; car, star,* and *jar.* Pick one up and have your child name it, then have him or her try to find an object that rhymes with the first one.

- Make animal noises and have your child guess the animal. Or reverse the roles and guess what animal your child is imitating. For some animals, your child can add actions, too.

Make Music a Part of Daily Life

Research indicates that exposure to music has numerous benefits for a child's development. Music promotes language acquisition, listening skills, memory, and motor skills.

- Play children's tapes in the car and at home. Fit songs into your daily routine, before and during mealtimes, and at bedtime. Select from musical recordings listed on pages 13 and 14.

- Encourage your child to feel the rhythm of the music. Dance, clap, and sway to the sounds. Join your toddler while watching quality children's videos—*A Young Children's Concert with Raffi* is great fun.

- Sing to your child and encourage your child to join in. Singing introduces words, nonsense sounds, rhymes, and rhythms, all in an enjoyable package.

- Share songbooks that you'll find on the following list. If you play guitar or piano, get a collection with musical notation to play while you and your child sing.

- Toddlers and preschoolers will also enjoy looking at illustrated versions of single songs in the list on pages 26 and 27, opening the flaps in the two movable books while singing along.

Recommended Songbooks

In this list are some collections with simple music for piano and guitar, which make excellent gifts that provide years of family singing.

Carter, David A. *If You're Happy and You Know It, Clap Your Hands: A Pop-Up Book.*
Your child will enjoy pulling tabs to make a chicken flap its wings, an owl wink, and other actions in this lively children's song.

Emerson, Sally, with music arranged by Mary Frank. *The Kingfisher Nursery Rhyme Songbook.* Illustrated by Colin and Moira Maclean.
One of the few large collections available, this valuable resource features forty songs with lyrics and music for piano and guitar.

Hillenbrand, Will. *Down by the Station.*
With the music notation for the catchy tune, this charming book about a train, with "the puffer-bellies all in a row," has inviting lyrics and pictures.

MacLeod, Elizabeth. *I Heard a Little Baa.* Illustrated by Louise Phillips.
This small book uses flaps effectively to create a guessing game that can be sung to the tune of "Farmer in the Dell."

Manning, Jane. *My First Songs.*
This supplies parents with several folk songs such as "Old MacDonald," "The Eentsy-Weentsy Spider," "Row, Row, Row Your Boat," and more.

Orozco, José-Luis. *De Colores and Other Latin-American Folk Songs for Children.* Illustrated by Elisa Kleven.
If you're looking for Spanish songs, here are twenty-seven songs in Spanish and English, with simple piano music and guitar chords, and wonderful pictures.

Paxton, Tom. *Going to the Zoo.* Illustrated by Karen Lee Schmidt.
Belt this out in the car on the way to the zoo or anywhere else. You and your child can add your own verses to the simple, toe-tapping song.

Raffi. *Raffi Children's Favorites.*
This large paperback collection is a gold mine of songs with musical notations, including Raffi's well-known hits and traditional favorites.

Taback, Simms. *I Know an Old Lady Who Swallowed a Fly.*
This silly, familiar folk song takes on a new life with award-winning illustrations that offer humor for adults as well as children.

Zelinsky, Paul O. *The Wheels on the Bus.*
This pop-up book has tabs, flaps, turning wheels, and whooshing windshield wipers that add another dimension to this popular song.

Activities to Help Your Child Learn About Letters

• Provide art materials for exploration. Toddlers love to play with dough, water, and shaving cream. Creating objects and shapes with art items helps develop small-muscle skills that are necessary to learn to print when the time comes.

• Notice and compliment your toddler when she creates pictures or letter-like symbols. Writing letters comes much later, but meanwhile celebrate these first attempts.

• Sing the alphabet song often.

• Place magnetic letters low on the refrigerator for easy access. Spell out your child's name and tell him the names of the letters.

• Point out letters in the environment. The *K* at Kmart and *STOP* on signs are sometimes the first letters a child learns.

Play Dough

 ½ cup salt
 1 cup flour
 1 tablespoon cream of tartar
 1 tablespoon oil
 1 cup water

Combine ingredients in a saucepan. Heat gently, stirring all the time. When the dough has a good consistency, take it off the heat and allow to cool.

Colored Play Dough

 2½ cups flour
 ½ cup salt
 2 packages unsweetened Kool-Aid
 2 cups boiling water
 3 tablespoons vegetable oil

Mix dry ingredients. Add water and oil; stir. Mix or knead with hands when cool. Store in a plastic bag or container with lid. Lasts for several months.

Activities to Promote Your Child's Awareness of Print

• Invite toddlers to help you with the grocery list. At the store, point out the items as you find them and have your toddler draw a line through a word.

• Make a flip book with close-up pictures of family members glued to small squares of poster board. Write the name in large letters under the picture. Put one face to a page, poke a hole in the corner, and secure with yarn. This is a book your child will read again and again.

• Read regularly to your toddler. Reading should always be a pleasurable experience, not a chore or required activity. Extend the book experience by asking open-ended questions like "Why do you think the duck flew away?" or "What can Sarah do to make her friend feel better?"

• Encourage your toddler to retell a story while looking at the pictures in a book. He can "read" the story to a favorite stuffed animal.

Recommended Books for Toddlers

While parents should keep reading nursery rhymes and small board books to this age group, it's also time to add bigger hardcover and paperback books that have more complicated pictures than most board books. Illustration styles vary more, with lots to choose from. This age group adores books with flaps they can open and books with parts that pop up.

Stories are also a bit more complicated for this age group, often with predictable patterns and phrases that invite the child to join in. Rhyming texts are still popular, but also look for stories with simple plotlines. Expect young listeners to want to participate by joining in fingerplays, naming animals and colors, and imitating animal and vehicle noises. They may even learn a story word for word and say it along with you, not allowing any changes or mistakes. Many toddlers want to hear the same story again and again, a request parents should indulge because it teaches vocabulary and story patterns.

As always, the goal is to have fun reading. If your child is learning colors and the names of objects, that's great. But the main emphasis should be on pleasurable time together.

Barton, Byron. *My Car.*
Eye-catching colors set against a cheerful yellow background introduce Sam and his red car in this outstanding book.

Brown, Margaret Wise. *Goodnight, Moon.* Illustrated by Clement Hurd.
The well-loved pictures and simple phrases of this bedtime favorite soothe listening children as a bunny says good night to its room.

Carle, Eric. *The Very Hungry Caterpillar.*
This modern classic starts with a little caterpillar who ends up as a beautiful butterfly. Great for toddlers and preschoolers.

Dunrea, Olivier. *Gossie.*
In this brilliantly simple book, a gosling named Gossie loses her favorite boots and finds them in an unexpected place. Followed by *Gossie & Gertie.*

Inkpen, Mick. *Wibbly Pig Likes Bananas.*
Pitched perfectly at young children, this small book shows Wibbly Pig making choices, then asks the listener to choose, too. One in a series.

Mayer, Mercer. *A Boy, a Dog, and a Frog.*
Add your own words to this funny story about a boy who tries to catch a self-satisfied frog. With delightful black-and-white illustrations and a surprise ending.

Newcome, Zita. *Toddlerobics.*
Eight toddlers in colorful gym clothes move in ways that toddlers will want to imitate.

Oxenbury, Helen. *I Touch.*
Roly-poly toddlers explore the world, encountering a colorful beach ball, a worm, and more. Look for the companion books *I Can, I Hear,* and *I See.*

Rathmann, Peggy. *Good Night, Gorilla.*
In this funny, nearly wordless book, a little gorilla takes a zookeeper's keys and lets the other animals out of their cages, to follow the unsuspecting zookeeper to his house.

Rosen, Michael. *We're Going on a Bear Hunt.*
Illustrated by Helen Oxenbury.
Take your child on an adventure with this upbeat book that combines engaging pictures and rhythmic words that invite listeners to join in.

Smith, Charles R., Jr. *Brown Sugar Babies.*
Eight irresistible, brown-skinned babies glow with pleasure and personality in close-ups and smaller photographs.

Yolen, Jane. *How Do Dinosaurs Say Good Night?*
Illustrated by Mark Teague.
This priceless, wonderfully illustrated book stars misbehaving dinosaurs who are trying to delay bedtime. Followed by *How Do Dinosaurs Get Well Soon?*

Gift Ideas for Toddlers

Active Play
- Low climber
- Play dough
- Bells, wood block, drum, triangle
- Large rubber balls
- Tricycle

Books and Music
- Picture books, stories, and poems about things children know
- Recordings of classical music, folk music, or children's songs

Art Supplies
- Wide-tip watercolor markers
- Large sheets of paper and an easel
- Finger paints or tempura paint, ½-inch brushes
- Blunt scissors
- White glue

Dolls and Pretend Play
- Washable dolls with clothes
- Doll beds
- Child-sized table and chairs

- Dishes, pots, and pans
- Dress-up clothes such as hats, shoes, and shirts
- Hand puppets
- Shopping cart

Manipulatives
- Wooden puzzles (four to twenty large pieces)
- Big beads or spools to string together
- Sewing cards
- Stacking toys
- Unit blocks and accessories

3

Preschoolers
Ages Three to Four

Few children learn to read books by themselves.
Someone has to lure them into the wonderful world
of the written word; someone has to show them the way.
—*Orville Prescott*

Preschool children, ages three to four, have vocabularies of five hundred to two thousand words. They understand what is said to them, can follow directions, and speak clearly enough to be understood. They ask endless questions, can relate past experiences, do simple rhyming, and love being read to. Play is preschoolers' work. They engage in hours of symbolic play. They take on the role of others (Dad, Mom, the doctor, or an animal) and create familiar settings (grocery store, a wedding) in which to pretend.

While children develop at somewhat different rates, experts offer overall milestones regarding literacy development. By age four, children typically listen to longer stories and can turn one page at a time, which they may insist on doing. Many can recite some nursery rhymes and sing a few songs completely. When looking at pictures in books, they can identify basic colors and shapes. They've become conversant with the idea of "let's pretend" and may act out familiar stories. They also find more things funny, and may make up silly words and stories—laughing profusely at their own humor.

The Get Ready to Read project of the National Center for Learning Disabilities offers a twenty-question screening tool for parents of four-year-olds at www.getreadytoread.org. The score indicates if the child's prereading skills are strong, weak, or somewhere in between. It's recommended that parents use the screening tool two or three times in the year before a child begins kindergarten. For children whose skills need improvement, the Web site provides activities and resources.

Activities to Promote Oral Language and Vocabulary

- Cooking and household chores are excellent opportunities for language development as well as building a sense of importance and confidence. Allow children to help put clothes away. Let them help you make cookies and other simple recipes. Explain new vocabulary words like *tablespoon, stir, blend, chop, mash, season, fry, bake, boil,* and *combine.*

- Share the fun of cooking with the wonderful cookbook *Pretend Soup and Other Real Recipes: A Cookbook for Preschoolers & Up* by Mollie Katzen and Ann Henderson.

- Visit the library regularly, where you'll find a great selection of books and other materials. Research indicates that children's books are a wonderful source of rare words. These are vocabulary words that we do not use in our daily conversations with children but are important for them to know, words such as *circus, parachute, jungle, reef, legend,* and *mermaid.*

Musical Recordings for Toddlers and Preschoolers

- Play musical recordings to inspire your child to listen, move, dance, and sing along. Songs introduce new words, often ones that rhyme or repeat, which makes them easy to learn. Try some of the recordings on the following list to play in the car or at home.

Boston Pops. *Classics for Kids.* **RCA.**
This well-chosen introduction to classical music includes pieces from the Nutcracker Suite, Carnival of the Animals, and more.

Ella Jenkins. *Come Dance by the Ocean.*
Smithsonian Folkways.
Songs that celebrate the environment combine with those that reinforce concepts, such as "Easy as ABC" and "Numbers and Alphabets."

Fred Koch. *Did You Feed My Cow?* **Melody House.**
This award winner takes the classic songs of Ella Jenkins and gives them a new twist, with lots of invitations for children to join in singing and swinging.

Justin Roberts. *Great Big Sun.*
Hear Diagonally Records.
Songs with a folksy style, about nature and family, fill this fresh recording.

Rachel Sumner. *I've Got Imagination*.
Rachel's Records.
Children will be moving and grooving to these songs, both original and traditional.

Joel Frankel. *JoJo the Scarecrow: Barnyard Bash*.
Digital Entertainment.
This excellent combination of language and music ranges from Dixieland to pop sounds, with songs built around the appealing topic of animals.

Raffi. *Let's Play*. Rounder.
From the traditional "If You're Happy and You Know It" to the pop hit "Yellow Submarine," this collection is another great offering by this favorite children's performer.

Jessica Harper. *Rhythm in My Shoes*. Rounder.
Known first as an actress, Harper has turned her talents to singing original songs, from chants to tongue twisters to child-friendly rap.

Kathy Reid-Naiman. *Say Hello to the Morning*.
Merriweather.
This selection of songs, rhymes, and singing games that invite children to join in comes with a booklet of lyrics and suggestions for parents.

Sweet Honey in the Rock. *Still the Same Me*. Rounder.
With wonderful harmonies from a popular singing group, this will have children singing and clapping along.

Activities to Promote Your Child's Awareness of the Sounds of Language

• Play the "I'm thinking of . . ." game in the car, on the bus, or whenever you have a few minutes to fill. You can focus on rhyming words or beginning sounds of words. For example, say, "I'm thinking of the name of an animal that rhymes with box." Or, "I'm thinking of things that are good to eat that start with *m-m-m*." (Say the sound, not the letter.)

• Play "Put It Together." In this oral game, you say the different sounds in a word slowly, separating them so that each sound is isolated. "What do you get when you put these sounds together: f-i-sh?" (Say the sounds, not the letters.) This is difficult for some children, but they enjoy listening closely and putting the sounds back together to make a word. Make it fun, play it often, and give them lots of help.

• Say tongue twisters as an enjoyable way to play with the sounds of language. Follow your child's lead and have fun with this game. Here are three simple ones to start with.
   • Tall Tammy took ten turkeys.
   • Silly Sam saw seven snakes.
   • Happy Harry had hamburgers.

- Try these two old favorites, and find more in *Busy Buzzing Bumblebees and Other Tongue Twisters*, a short, illustrated book by Alvin Schwartz.
  - Sally sells seashells by the seashore.
  - Peter Piper picked a peck of pickled peppers.

- Read rhyming books like those suggested in the following list. Here are three approaches:
  - First read the book with your child a couple of times simply for pleasure.
  - Read the book again, but this time stop when you come to a word that rhymes with a previous word. Ask your child what word might rhyme and make sense in the story. If he doesn't know, just tell him and point out what rhyming sounds like, stressing the ending sounds.
  - On another occasion, ask the child to listen for words in the story that start with the same sound.

Books That Encourage Sound Awareness

While all well-written books help children to acquire language, books such as the ones on this list especially encourage listeners to join in with the words. Many of these stories use rhymes that make it easy for a preschooler to complete the sentence if they've heard it before. Others use repetition, and children start listening for the repeated word or phrase and joining in. When you're reading a familiar book aloud, start pausing if your child seems about to say the next word. For example, in *The Lady with the Alligator Purse,* a repeated phrase that invites participation is "In came the doctor, in came the nurse, and in came the lady with the alligator purse." Within a few readings, some children will be eager to supply the final "lady with the alligator purse."

Charlip, Remy. *Fortunately.*
When Ned gets invited to a faraway birthday party, a zany adventure begins that combines fortunate and unfortunate events.

Degen, Bruce. *Jamberry.*
A rollicking, rhyming story about a boy and bear buried neck high in berries, dancing in them, playing with them, and eating them. A real jamboree.

Guarino, Deborah. *Is Your Mama a Llama?*
Illustrated by Steven Kellogg.
A rhyming book that is also a guessing game, this will have
preschoolers shouting out animal names.

Keats, Ezra Jack. *Over in the Meadow.*
This folk counting rhyme has the polished rhythm of oral
tradition and unusually lovely pictures.

Marshall, James. *Old Mother Hubbard and Her
Wonderful Dog.*
A favorite old rhyme illustrated with hilarious pictures.

Martin, Bill, Jr., and John Archambault. *Chicka Chicka
Boom Boom.* **Illustrated by Lois Ehlert.**
This terrific book introduces the alphabet with toe-tapping
verses and bright, clever pictures. (Look for the original version, not the shortened board book.)

McPhail, David. *Pigs Aplenty, Pigs Galore.*
This energetic story is as fun to read aloud as it is to listen
to, as a group of pigs arrive and throw an unexpected, exuberant party.

Pomerantz, Charlotte. *The Piggy in the Puddle.*
Illustrated by James Marshall.
"Mud is squishy, mud is squashy / Mud is oh so squishy
squashy," reads one of the verses in this terrific story that's
full of wordplay.

Seuss, Dr. *Hop on Pop.*
Children of all ages enjoy this Seuss classic, which hops energetically along, full of rhymes, wordplay, and zany characters.

Shaw, Nancy. *Sheep in a Jeep.*
Illustrated by Margot Apple.
Wonderful for a wide range of ages, this rhyming story opens, "Beep! Beep! / Sheep in a jeep on a hill that's steep," and continues in the same upbeat vein.

Sierra, Judy. *Tasty Baby Belly Buttons.*
Illustrated by Meilo So.
In this Japanese folktale, a couple find a baby in a watermelon and name her Uriko. She ends up a heroine, in a story told with rhythmic phrases children love to repeat.

Wilson, Karma. *Bear Snores On.*
Illustrated by Jane Chapman.
The short rhyming verses in this large book about a sleeping bear dance the listener along, only slowing the pace for the repeated phrase "But the bear snores on."

Simple Play Activities for Preschoolers

Research shows that young children learn through exploration and play. They need lots of time to interact with the world physically, using their senses. The sense of touch in these simple activities teaches them about their surroundings while they enjoy a good time.

Water play. Provide your child with a large tub of water or a wading pool, or use the bathtub. Let your child experiment with pouring water into and through various containers, exploring what floats and what sinks, wetting and squeezing cloths and sponges, and so on. Here are some items to have on hand:

- Plastic cups of different sizes (poke holes in one of the cups to make a "rainmaker")
- Plastic bottles
- Plastic tubing
- Funnels
- Bulb baster
- Sponges and washcloths

Remember that water play requires adult supervision.

Sand play. Like water play, playing in sand lends itself to lots of containers for mixing, measuring, pouring, and molding. Have water on hand to mix with the sand. Supply your child with items like these:

- Cups of different sizes
- Sieves
- Measuring spoons
- Funnels
- Small shovels and other implements
- Containers that can mold the sand into shapes

Keep in mind that getting dirty is a welcome by-product of playing!

Mystery object game. Assemble items your child knows well, like a spoon, brush, cup, keys, and familiar small toys. Put them in a bag, and let your child reach into the bag and feel them one by one. See if your child can name the item before pulling it out to check. You can vary the game by saying "Can you find the spoon?"

Activities to Help Your Child Learn About Letters

- Read ABC books. These books present each letter of the alphabet song with pictures of items that begin with the letter sound. Reading these books not only increases vocabulary, it also provides opportunities for learning activities. Here are a few of the many alphabet books available:
    - *26 Letters and 99 Cents* by Tana Hoban
    - *Eating the Alphabet: Fruits and Vegetables from A to Z* by Lois Ehlert
    - *John Burningham's ABC* by John Burningham

- As you read, frequently repeat the alphabet up to that point, and ask your child what comes next: "ABCDE-FGHI . . . what will be on the next page? Let's see what letter it is. OPQRS . . . what letter is next?"

- Provide your child with art and writing supplies such as washable markers, chalk, crayons, gluing items, and a variety of paper in different sizes, colors, and textures. Let them draw to their heart's content and make first attempts at writing.

- Give your child opportunities to handle alphabet items such as magnetic letters, sponge letters, and letters shaped out of pipe cleaners. Some children learn best when they have something physical to touch.

Helping Children "Write" at Home

- Help your child make greeting cards for grandparents and other relatives. Cut out pictures from old cards to make new cards by decorating folded construction paper.

- Making journals or books out of simple shapes is one way to motivate children. Just fold several sheets of paper in half, staple, and cut into an apple, house, or any other shape your child will enjoy.

- Have your child pretend to write grocery lists, phone messages, and notes to relatives, just like you do. It won't look like writing yet, but it will make them feel grown up, and they'll start to understand the many uses of print.

- Blackboards, whiteboards, and magic slates provide chances for children to practice a combination of beginning writing and drawing called "driting."

- Early scribbling, drawing, and writing should be encouraged and celebrated. These beginning attempts with pens, pencils, and crayons prepare children in an unpressured way for later success in reading and writing.

- Keep a shoe box full of scrap paper, envelopes, junk mail, crayons, scissors, glue, and writing tools. Having everything in one place makes it easier for your children to draw, copy, or paste.

- During the summer, allow children to paint with water on sidewalks or fences using large brushes.

- Help children write their name with pipe cleaners, magnets, or play dough.

Activities to Promote Your Child's Awareness of Print

- Support your child's interest in letters of the alphabet in her environment. Letters all around are a natural place to start learning. Emphasize the first letter of your child's name. For a child named Jane, *J* is a very special letter. Have her search for *J*'s, looking on cereal boxes and in magazines. Let her cut letters out and glue them down on a *J* page, with a photo of her on it.

- Help your child notice, describe, and create patterns. While playing with blocks, point out the pattern of one large and two small blocks that may be in a wall she is building. On a child's shirt, point out the repetition of colors: red, blue, yellow; red, blue, yellow. Using patterns helps us learn to organize information. When a child's brain absorbs and stores patterns, it enhances learning.

- Write, write, write. Lists, letters, stories, and books of any sort are wonderful ways to help children understand that the printed word is just the spoken word written down.

- Make a special family picture book for your child. Use photos of family members and write their names beneath the pictures. If aunts, uncles, grandmas, and grandpas don't live nearby, your child can look at the picture while talking on the phone and make a visual connection.

- Create a personal ABC book with your child. Make it as fancy or plain as you like.
  - Start with a spiral notebook, designate a page for each letter, and write a capital and small letter at the top.
  - Include anything that you want on the page that starts with that letter. Glue down photos of pictures cut from magazines, or have your child draw pictures.
  - Print the name of the object with your child. Say each letter as you write it.
  - Pages don't need to be done in alphabetical order.
  - The result will be a special book for you and your child to share.

Recommended Books for Preschoolers

The choice in books expands greatly by the time your child reaches this age group. You have so much to choose from, with wonderful pictures and engaging stories, that many parents find it helpful to check out a stack of books from their public library to find ones their children love. Your child might be developing preferences, too, for specific series, such as *George and Martha,* or types of books, such as those with photographs or lots of information. Keep reading familiar, well-loved books, but add in new ones, too.

Plots get more complicated as children get older, and illustrations become more detailed. You may spend more time than before talking about a book and looking at the pictures with your child. Expect to read certain books again and again, and to read them word for word, with no changes allowed by an alert listener. Many children this age pretend to read familiar books, which reflects their knowledge of how books work, how pages turn, and the way stories unfold.

Parents are often delighted to realize how clever and funny these books are. So have a good time, and your child will, too.

Brown, Margaret Wise. *Runaway Bunny.*
Illustrated by Clement Hurd.
When a bunny describes how he will run away from home, his mother explains how she will keep him in sight. By the team who created *Goodnight Moon.*

George, Kristine O'Connell. *Book!*
Illustrated by Maggie Smith.
A plump-faced, brown-skinned young child enjoys a new book, pretending to read it to the cat, upside down, alone, to a baby sibling, and with Mother.

Henkes, Kevin. *Chester's Way.*
The brave mouse Lilly rescues her friends from bullies, teaches them how to do wheelies, and *always* carries a loaded squirt gun. Everyone should meet her!

Horenstein, Henry. *Arf! Beg! Catch! Dogs from A to Z.*
Children who love dogs or prefer "real pictures" will love this alphabet of dog photographs.

Marshall, James. *George and Martha.*
Here is the first in a series of incomparable stories with great pictures about two hippos who are good friends but have the ups and downs of all friendships.

Meddaugh, Susan. *Martha Speaks.*
When Martha the dog eats vegetable soup, she starts to speak, and her new talent saves the day in an unexpected way.

Pinkney, Brian. *JoJo's Flying Side Kick.*
In order to earn her yellow belt in tae kwon do, JoJo must break a board with a flying side kick. With the help of her family, she masters her fears and succeeds.

Rathmann, Peggy. *Officer Buckle and Gloria.*
Officer Buckle and his dog, Gloria, visit schools to give safety tips, which Gloria demonstrates comically behind the unsuspecting officer's back.

Shannon, David. *No, David!*
Although David means well, he is such a handful that his mother is constantly saying, "No, David." Children—and many adults—will enjoy his naughtiness.

Slobodkina, Esphyr. *Caps for Sale: A Tale of a Peddler, Some Monkeys and Their Monkey Business.*
This time-tested picture book about a man and some mischievous monkeys is a delight to read aloud, with refrains and actions that invite children to join in.

Waddell, Martin. *Can't You Sleep, Little Bear?*
Illustrated by Barbara Firth.
In a soothing bedtime tale, Little Bear can't sleep, so his gentle father takes him outside to see the moon and stars.

Yolen, Jane. *Owl Moon.* **Illustrated by John Schoenherr.**
With exquisite watercolors, this award-winning book takes children on a magical walk through the winter woods to watch for owls.

Gift Ideas for Preschoolers

Dolls and Pretend Play
• Dolls and accessories
• Doll carriage
• Child-sized stove or sink
• Dress-up clothes
• Play food and cardboard cartons
• Dollhouse with accessories
• Finger or stick puppets

Manipulatives
• Puzzles and pegboards
• Large and small beads to string together
• Flannel board with pictures and letters
• Block shapes

Active Play
• Plastic bats and balls
• Water toys such as measuring cups and eggbeaters
• Sand toys such as muffin tins and toy vehicles
• Potter's clay
• Bowling pins, ring toss, and beanbags

Books and Music
• Simple science books
• More detailed picture-story books
• Sturdy tape player
• Recordings of a wide variety of music
• Books that come with a cassette recording

Art Supplies
• Easel, narrow brushes, and paint
• Thick crayons and chalk
• Paste and tape with dispenser
• Collage materials for gluing onto paper

4

Learning Disabilities

Those who do not develop the pleasure reading habit
simply don't have a chance—they will have a very difficult
time reading and writing at a level high enough to deal
with the demands of today's world.
—*Stephen Krashen*

Experts estimate that one in five children has a learning
disability, a general term that refers to different learning
problems. These can include difficulty with reading,
writing, speaking, listening, reasoning, and doing math.
Different children experience different problems or
combinations of problems. These come from differences
in how their brains function and how they process information, not from laziness or low intelligence. In fact,
children with learning disabilities tend to be of average
intelligence or above.

Although such problems can't be "cured" in the sense that they will disappear, children can learn ways to compensate for the difficulties and become successful learners.

The following list gives signs that may indicate learning disabilities. If your child displays regular patterns of these characteristics, have him evaluated. Early intervention can make a big difference in his ability to succeed in school. The Web sites listed later in this chapter also offer useful information for parents.

If you suspect your child may have a learning disability, there is assistance available to you under the federal Individuals with Disabilities Education Act (IDEA). Contact your school district for information on the free preschool screening evaluation that is offered in all school districts. If this evaluation indicates a possible learning disability, further evaluation and intervention may be recommended.

Warning Signs of Learning Disabilities

Language Development
Your child has difficulty:

- Learning the alphabet, colors, and shapes
- Pronouncing words
- Rhyming words
- Connecting sounds and letters
- Counting and learning numbers
- Being understood when speaking
- Following simple directions
- Expressing wants or needs
- Putting words together into phrases (uses words out of sequence)
- Understanding directions

Social Development
Your child:

- Prefers to play by himself and doesn't make friends easily
- Is overly aggressive or withdrawn
- Cries frequently and/or has sudden mood swings
- Becomes overly upset when frustrated

Attention Span
Your child:

- Has a short attention span
- Acts before thinking
- Becomes easily distracted

Physical Development
Your child has difficulty:

- Using scissors, pencils, and crayons
- With balance and coordination
- Focusing
- Making sense of what he sees

Web Sites About Learning Disabilities

- National Center on Learning Disabilities: www.ld.org
  An information-packed site about dealing with learning disabilities, with advice for children, teens and adults. One useful feature leads to resources in each state.
- Get Ready to Read: www.getreadytoread.org
  Offers a helpful screening tool for parents of four-year-olds to assess their pre-reading skills, and provides activities and resources to strengthen those skills.
- Schwab Foundation: www.schwablearning.org
  A parents' guide for helping children with learning disabilities. The Web site gives information about identifying learning disabilities, steps parents can take, and useful resources.
- Lee Pesky Learning Center: www.lplearningcenter.org
  Provides information about the center's services and resources.
- WETA, Washington, D.C., in association with The Coordinated Campaign for Learning Disabilities provides www.ldonline.org, a resource for parents, teachers, and other professionals.
- Stern Center for Language Learning: www.sterncenter.org
- All Kinds of Minds: www.allkindsofminds.org
  Information and resources for families, educators, and other professionals.

5

Resources for Parents

The single most important activity for building the
knowledge required for eventual success in reading is
reading aloud to children.
—*Carol Chomsky*

Tips on How and When to Read Aloud

- If you're not used to reading aloud, don't worry. A baby or young child is the perfect audience, eager to hear your voice and watch your face.
- Fit reading into different parts of your child's day. Prop up a book of nursery rhymes to read from when changing diapers or feeding your baby.

- Read before naptime and bedtime, but also read bouncier books when your child is feeling active and can move along with the book's rhythm.

- Bring books with you wherever you go—in the car, to the doctor's, to a relative's house. Keep books in diaper bags, cars, and purses.

- Have a special place for your growing child to keep books; make sure he or she can reach it easily. (Keep special books you hope to preserve on a higher shelf.)

- Try to read books you are excited about or your child is excited about. Expect to read the same book many times if your child likes it.

- Read with expression. Sometimes get louder, then softer. Vary your voice when a character is speaking.

- You might sometimes speed up at an exciting moment, but usually read at a moderate pace, not too fast. Your child needs time to digest the words and story.

- Feel free to stop and talk sometimes. Answer questions as they come up. Stop to enjoy the pictures, too.

- Remember: toddlers and preschoolers can act restless and still be listening. If they're enjoying the book, let them squirm and play with toys as they listen.

- If your child is not enjoying a book, you don't have to finish it.

- You don't have to read a book word for word, especially if your toddler is turning the pages too quickly for you to keep up.

- Reading aloud is highly educational, but it works best if you don't give that any thought. Your goal is *not* to teach your child to read, but to have fun together with books.

A child who loves books will be eager to read when the time comes.

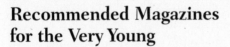

Recommended Magazines for the Very Young

Getting magazines in the mail is an exciting event for children. Magazines can be wonderful springboards for reading, discussion, and activities.

Babybug
For ages six months to two years, this has high-quality stories, poems, and illustrations. More information at www.cricketmag.com.

Click
A science and exploration magazine for ages two to six. More information at www.cricketmag.com.

Ladybug
For ages two to six years. From the same publisher as *Babybug,* this is another high-quality magazine with excellent stories and pictures.

Wild Animal Baby
A nature magazine for ages one to three, with good color photographs. From the National Wildlife Federation, www.nwf.org.

Your Big Backyard
For ages three to seven, this focuses on nature, especially wild animals. More information at www.nwf.org.

Recommended Caldecott Award Winners and Honor Books

One of the great pleasures of children's books are the wonderful illustrations, which will probably be your child's first introduction to art. Terrific illustrators have turned their talents to making these books a pleasure, using a whole range of art styles. While many books have good pictures, you can also seek out books like those on this list, which have won awards for their illustrations. Each year, the American Library Association gives the Caldecott Medal to a book notable for its artwork, and Caldecott Honor Awards to other books with distinguished art. Here are some Caldecott books that suit young children.

Bang, Molly. *Ten, Nine, Eight.*
A small, dark-skinned girl and her father count down together from ten to one, starting with her ten toes and ending with "1 big girl all ready for bed."

Crews, Donald. *Freight Train.*
Striking graphics and vibrant colors show a freight train picking up speed as it travels through the countryside, first in light and then in darkness as night comes on.

Ehlert, Lois. *Color Zoo.*
Clever die-cut shapes form different animals, inviting children to name the animals, shapes, and colors.

Fleming, Denise. *In a Small, Small Pond.*
Lovely, textured illustrations combine with a jaunty text in this trip to a pond where a new animal appears on every page.

Keats, Ezra Jack. *The Snowy Day.*
Don't miss this stellar, timeless book with collage illustrations about a young boy enjoying a walk on a snowy day.

McCloskey, Robert. *Make Way for Ducklings.*
Parents may remember the old-fashioned, appealing black-and-white illustrations of this charming story about a family of ducks in Boston.

Sendak, Maurice. *Where the Wild Things Are.*
With flawless pacing and well-loved pictures, this modern classic follows a boy named Max to a magic land, where he meets the wild things, and then back home again.

Tafuri, Nancy. *Have You Seen My Duckling?*
"Have you seen my duckling?" a mother duck asks various animals, while her little duck hides somewhere in the large, graceful illustrations.

Wiesner, David. *Tuesday.*
In this entertaining, nearly wordless book, surprised frogs find themselves flying through a neighborhood, stopping to watch a little television, and having a great time.

Williams, Vera B. *"More, More, More," Said the Baby: 3 Love Stories.*
Large, lushly colored illustrations tell three stories about toddlers and the adults who love them and play with them.

Wood, Audrey. *King Bidgood's in the Bathtub.*
Illustrated by Don Wood.
A king eats, fishes, and enjoys the day in a magical tub, depicted in superb pictures.

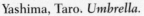

Yashima, Taro. *Umbrella.*
Bon polo, bon polo, ponpolo ponpolo beats the rain on Momo's new umbrella in this wonderful story about a young Asian American girl growing up in a city.

Books in Spanish for Young Children

Since so many families speak Spanish, here is a short list of books for young children in Spanish, either translated from English or with Spanish and English printed side-by-side. All have wonderful illustrations and are a pleasure to read. To find more titles, check the Web site of the Association for Library Service to Children, a division of the American Library Association (www.ala.org).

Brown, Margaret Wise. *El Gran Granero Rojo* (Big Red Barn).

Browne, Anthony. *Cosas Que Me Gustan* (Things I Like).

Delacre, Lulu. *Arroz con Leche: Popular Songs and Rhymes from Latin America.*

Frasier, Debra. *El Día en Que Tú Naciste* (On the Day You Were Born).

Galdone, Paul. *Los Tres Chivitos Gruff* (The Three Billy Goats Gruff).

Griego, Margot C. *Tortillitas Para Mamá and Other Nursery Rhymes: Spanish and English.*

Jaramillo, Nelly Palacio. *Las Nanas de Abuelita* (Grandmother's Nursery Rhymes).

Keats, Ezra Jack. *La Silla de Pedro* (Peter's Chair).

McBratney, Sam. *¿Adivina Cuánto Te Quiero?* (Guess How Much I Love You).

McDonnell, Flora. *Quiero a Los Animales* (I Love Animals).

Seuss, Dr. *Huevos Verdes con Jamón* (Green Eggs and Ham).
Zion, Gene. *Harry, el Perrito Sucio* (Harry the Dirty Dog).

Resources at Your Public Library

Public libraries are a great resource for parents. They are free and typically offer a broader and deeper range of books than bookstores do. Before buying a book, try checking out a lot of books and finding the ones your child loves. Get to know a children's librarian who can steer you to wonderful books and other helpful resources. Here are just a handful of what many public libraries offer:

- Storytimes for toddlers and preschoolers, and in many cases for infants. Learn about new books and fingerplays while your child is entertained. You can also meet other parents who value books.
- Musical CDs or cassettes, and recordings of children's books to check out.
- Videotapes and DVDs (use these sparingly—children need human interaction and physical play, not just passive viewing).
- Parenting books on child development, education, and more.
- Computerized catalogs that make it easy to find books and borrow them from other libraries. Many library catalogs can be accessed from home through the Internet.
- Access to the Internet, which itself has many parenting resources.

Organizations and Web Sites Concerned with Young Children

Association of Library Services to Children
(a division of the American Library Association)
www.ala.org/alsc/born.html
Lots of useful information and links for parents, including book lists, lists of recommended recordings, and advice on reading to the very young.

Best Children's Music *www.bestchildrensmusic.com*
Find lists of recommended music recordings organized by age groups, with links to reviews and information about awards.

Early Childhood *www.earlychildhood.com*
This Web site brings together information on lots of subjects for parents and educators.

Get Ready to Read *www.getreadytoread.org*
A good source for early literacy activities for parents and teachers.

I Am Your Child *www.iamyourchild.org*
This advocacy group's Web site has tips and advice for parents of young children.

National Association for the Education of Young Children *www.naeyc.org*
This professional organization of early childhood educators provides a list of all early childhood programs that they accredit.

Parents as Teachers *www.patnc.org*
Offers lots of information and activities for parents.

Read to Me *www.readtomeprogram.org*
Look for the helpful frequently asked questions on reading
to the very young.

Zero to Three *www.zerotothree.org*
This Web site offers helpful information and resources for
parents and caregivers.

Recommended Books for Parents

Here are some useful and interesting books about babies, toddlers, books, and language that parents might
like to read if they have time.

Golinkoff, Roberta Michnick, and Kathy Hirsh-Pasek.
*How Babies Talk: The Magic and Mystery of Language
in the First Three Years of Life.*
A fascinating in-depth look at how babies and toddlers acquire language.

Gopnik, Alison, Andrew N. Meltzoff, and Patricia Kuhl.
*The Scientist in the Crib: Minds, Brains, and How
Children Learn.*
Discusses the latest information about how babies and tod-
dlers learn.

Rand, Donna, Toni Trent Parker, and Sheila Foster.
*Black Books Galore: Guide to Great African American
Children's Books.*
A terrific guide to books with African American characters,
for babies through ninth graders.

Odean, Kathleen. *Great Books for Babies and Toddlers: More Than 500 Recommended Books for Your Child's First Three Years.*
The only guide of its kind to help parents find the best books for young children. For books for ages three and older, consult the companion guides, *Great Books for Girls, Great Books for Boys,* and *Great Books About Things Kids Love.*

Oppenheim, Joanne, and Stephanie Oppenheim. *Toy Portfolio, 2004: The Best Toys, Books, Videos, Music & Software for Kids.*
This handy guide comes out every year with advice on toys, books, and media for children.

Shonkoff, Jack P., editor. *From Neurons to Neighborhoods: The Science of Early Childhood Development.*
Covers new research about early childhood development and the effects of a child's environment.

About the Lee Pesky Learning Center

THE LEE PESKY LEARNING CENTER was founded in Boise, Idaho, in 1997 by the Alan and Wendy Pesky family as a memorial to their son Lee. We began our work with providing services to students with learning disabilities. Alan Pesky's belief that each individual who walks through our doors is our most important client guides our growth. Direct services to learning-disabled students remains the core of our work.

We quickly became involved in developing research-based literacy curricula and providing professional staff development for educators. The staff of the Lee Pesky Learning Center is extensively involved in public and private reading initiatives—Idaho's Reading First under No Child Left Behind and The Open Book Initiative of the J. A. and Kathryn Albertson Foundation. Primary grant funding from the Dumke Foundation, with the assistance of the Idaho Community Foundation and the Whittenberg Foundation, supported the design and piloting of an early literacy curriculum for child care, day care, and preschool teachers.

Boise, Idaho, was the site for "The Beginnings" (Federal Literacy Summit for the Northwest Regions) in June 2002. The Lee Pesky Learning Center partnered with Idaho's First Lady Patricia Kempthorne and First Lady Laura Bush to con-

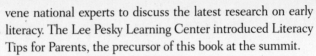

vene national experts to discuss the latest research on early literacy. The Lee Pesky Learning Center introduced Literacy Tips for Parents, the precursor of this book at the summit.

For more information on the summit, all of the Lee Pesky Learning Center's programs and research on literacy development, visit www.lplearningcenter.org.